The Poetry Apothecary

The Poetry Apothecary

Poems by

Cristina M. R. Norcross

© 2024 Cristina M. R. Norcross. All rights reserved.
This material may not be reproduced in any form, published,
reprinted, recorded, performed, broadcast,
rewritten, or redistributed without
the explicit permission of Cristina M. R. Norcross.
All such actions are strictly prohibited by law.

Cover design by Shay Culligan
Cover image by Kim Nelson
Author photo by Christopher Norcross

ISBN: 978-1-63980-641-6
Library of Congress Control Number: 2024944433

Kelsay Books
502 South 1040 East, A-119
American Fork, Utah 84003
Kelsaybooks.com

In memory of my father, Roger William Raskopf (1936–2020)

*

Rarely, if ever, are any of us healed in isolation.
Healing is an act of communion.
—bell hooks

The movement of grace is what changes us,
heals us and heals our world.
To summon grace, say, Help, and then buckle up.
Grace finds you exactly where you are,
but it doesn't leave you where it found you.
—Anne Lamott

Acknowledgments

I would like to extend a special thank you to the literary magazines, journals, anthologies, and other venues where some of the poems from *The Poetry Apothecary* were first published:

The Ekphrastic Review: "A Lemon Light Embrace," "Disappearing Ghosts Dancing"

GAS: Poetry, Art and Music: "The Salt That Remains"

Lothlorien Poetry Journal: "Sacred Stones of Loss," "Solar Eclipse Picnic," "You Are Earth"

Movement: Our Bodies in Motion (Sweetycat Press Anthology): "Dancing"

The Poet: "We Carry Tiny Planets of Love"

Silver Birch Press: "How to Stay Grounded in Times of Flux"

The Sound of a Collective Pulse (Kelsay Books): "Uncertain Feet"

Verse-Virtual: "Hay Bale Awakenings," "Stepping into the Greening Moments," "The Gathering of Sustenance"

Visual Verse: "Becoming Sundials," "When We Open the Next Door," "Winged Secrets in the Chest," "Your Story Sings Through Me"

Wednesday Night Poetry (WNP): "A House Under Violet Skies," "In Search of Tiny Forest Gods," "When You Hear Ada Limón Read a Poem"

Wisconsin Sijo Competition / 1st Place (sponsored by the Sejong Cultural Society and UW-Madison): "Capturing Light"

Writing in a Woman's Voice: "Catching Feathers," "Reading from the Songbook of Self"

Contents

Rx for Getting Lost and Being Found

A Solar Eclipse Picnic	17
Touching Tomorrow	18
A House Under Violet Skies	19
What We Sing into Existence	20
Becoming Sundials	21
Reading from the Songbook of Self	23
Thursdays at Café Rosie Lee	25
Disappearing Ghosts Dancing	27
Polished Pearl	28

Rx for Nourishment

Breathing in Tomorrow's Gold	31
Every Moment	33
The Gathering of Sustenance	34
Every Small Taste of Life	35
The Gentle Holy	36
Slow Motion Peace	37
Sacred Pause	38
Catching Feathers	39
What I Packed for You	41
Newfound Lungs	42
Rest Here in My Chest	43
Infinite and Holy	44
Marbled Glory, a Meditation	45
Double Helix Hope	46

Rx for Healing

A Painted Kiss	49
In Search of Tiny Forest Gods	50

Sound Healing	51
Rain Museum	52
Where Tender Truth Sings	53
These Things We Hold	54
How to Stay Grounded in Times of Flux	55
When You Hear Ada Limón Read a Poem	57
The Stillness of Enough	58
A Thousand Notes with Wings	59
White Light and Lava	60
A Salve	61

Rx for Raising Humans

When Our Son Became a Magpie	65
On the Edge of Next	67
Seeing Your Own Gold	68
The Cloak of Memory	69
Inviting New Songs	70
We Carry Tiny Planets of Love	72
Tashmoo Beach Smiles	73
Winged Secrets in the Chest	74
Sifting	76
Where My Curved Arms Arch	77
Time Traveling with Planets	79

Rx for Grief Work

Sacred Stones of Loss	83
A River of Blessings	84
The Salt That Remains	85
Stepping into the Greening Moments	87
The Space My Father Filled	88
Your Story Sings Through Me	89

When Sorrow Is Untidy	90
Open Your Eyes	91
When We Open the Next Door	92
Capturing Light	94
Things That Float from One Realm to the Next	95
A Shared Rest	97
Everything Becomes Again	98
A Twilight Glimpse	99
Coming Up Roses	100

Rx for Inspiration

Hay Bale Awakenings	103
Dancing	104
With Stones in Her Mouth	105
To Greet Each Moment with Awakening	106
I Rise to Meet Her Wings	107
Chocolate Chips Straight from the Bag	108
Gold Dust	109
To Uncurl Roots	110

Rx for Connection

A Tattooed Promise	113
A Lemon Light Embrace	114
You Are Earth	115
Slumber Song	116
Uncertain Feet	117
A Love Song in the Key of Blue	118
A Split Second Embrace	119
Life Becomes	120

Rx for Getting Lost and Being Found

A Solar Eclipse Picnic

We left the quiet dark,
the espresso café with tiny cups
and chess board tables,
to venture into sunlight,
climbing a path to the open green
of Parliament Hill.
In the broad, bright sky,
kites were flashing their tails,
winking at us.
Red and white blankets were spread out
for barefoot picnics.
We brought our own luncheon feast,
snuggled side by side on the nearest bench.

I remember the wind
whipping my hair into a frenzy,
napkins flying out of my hands,
an errant chip falling on the grass.
Absorbed in the conversation of
what comes next,
what comes after Ottawa,
a solar eclipse shadow
swept across the city like a giant condor.
We hardly felt time pass.
Finally, the jolt of a foreign, noonday chill
took our breath away,
as if these past 4 years had been swept up,
hidden inside the smoldering sun.
Unknown skies awaited us
on a different Parliament green,
on the other side of the ocean,
on the other side of now.

Touching Tomorrow

The sandhill cranes
will change their address soon,
leave the marshland behind our house
in search of cover from climate.
The peonies have already lost their pink petals
months before.
Nature embraces this letting go,
how this, too, is a kind of love.
The rest of us spin in circles,
water our gardens of hearth
and all that is familiar,
hoping for a rare renewal
of the current season.

I imagine transparent blooms
at the end of my fingertips,
how touching tomorrow
might make it grow inside of me.
I swallow the calendar,
wash it down with a mug of Zen tea,
accept that each, new day
will be slightly different,
a practice in praise,
believing in undiscovered moments,
that everything will be okay
in our family's migration
to an altered state—
its new found shape.

A House Under Violet Skies

My limbs, cells,
the delicate bones of the feet
all hold me up,
keep me standing.
Pulsing colors of deep burgundy
and sage green emerge,
a vibration I once knew more intimately,
before the forgetting
that comes with school,
social conventions, expectations.

There was a weeping willow tree
I once loved when I was six.
I used to sit underneath it,
using the branches as cover,
safely enclosed in the loving arms
of willow fronds,
soft and gentle, like breath.

I was scaffolding beneath tree structure,
an ever changing sky.
Nature housed me then.
Hidden, I looked out with pond frog eyes.

Stepping into moonlight
and morning song,
I realize that I am now the house,
a little stone cottage with eager vines
spiraling up the sides,
a steadying force
for the soul uncaged,
winging my way
to violet skies beyond.

What We Sing into Existence

I carry a parachute in my lungs,
so that hope will expand
and lift me off my feet,
growing an apple of promise
in my honey crisp heart.

I sing the buzz of energetic bees
every morning,
when my eyes glow golden with
the rising globe sun,
when morning sits on my chest,
like a contented cat claiming me.

Unfettered, the ghosts of past days
now leave me.
I am Cleopatra,
obsidian eyes surveying the land,
possessing gifts of survival—
acceptance, breath, the ability
to make things new,
singing them into existence,
one threaded stitch at a time,
carrying hope.

Becoming Sundials

inspired by an image by John Crozier

I am trimming my life back,
taking a train away
from cluttered expectations.
Maybe all I need can be carried in a single bag,
a backpack, hands-free,
walking towards some as of yet
unknown destination.

I remember taking the tube into London,
walking up and down Charing Cross Road,
lingering inside the Silver Moon Women's Bookshop,
my fingers touching titles,
choosing a slim volume of poetry
to read with a cheap cup of coffee
(that I would make last).
Back then, the dream was to expand,
expand from a one-bedroom flat to a house,
expand from a couple to a family,
fill space and time with plans,
more furniture,
a second fry pan.

With birds leaving the nest,
soon we will look to condense,
let go of large boxes,
duplicate kitchenware,
and too many sweaters.
Perhaps London will welcome us back,
at least for a visit,
tube train doors opening and closing,
the world now changed,
our swift feet a bit slower,

hands held, arms swinging,
with no need for destinations or plans,
just a cup of tea,
a willingness to let time pass like molasses,
the rushing of pulse
slowed to the sound of passing minutes,
our bodies unmoving sundials
on Hampstead Heath.

Reading from the Songbook of Self

inspired by Woman Reading in a Garden *by Mary Cassatt*

When I transferred schools,
moved up to Canada
and switched majors,
I discovered a garden within me.
I found Margaret Atwood,
Margaret Laurence,
Alice Munro.
Their words were blooms in my ears.
My world unfurled, opened up
to these wordsmiths of the North.
My hands became green leaves,
new shoots of ideas reaching out,
sprouting, turning pages.
Mesmerized by Atwood's characters surfacing,
entranced by Laurence's divining rod of truth,
I, too, was coming to the surface,
finding my own words
in the rich soil of experience.

I scoured used bookstores,
sat in the reading nook of the library window,
scribbled found thoughts on the bench
near Parliament Hill,
found myself in cups of tea
and blank notebooks,
took meditative walks
through ocean waves of snow.
My quiet sanctuary was an 8-hour drive
from the life I once knew.
I was recreating the self, becoming,
one page at a time, one paragraph at a time.

Holding the knowledge of tomorrow
on my tongue like a salted caramel square,
I held the book of me
close to my beating chest,
hearing music play,
as if for the very first time.

Thursdays at Café Rosie Lee

The sound of books closing, pens retracting
and backpacks zippering
signals the close of another academic day—
the beginning of Thursdays at Café Rosie Lee.

Taking three steps down into a cavern of warm, garlic heat
and the taste of creamed mushroom soup,
brings me effortlessly to my once-a-week world
of food, friendship, and Sangria.

We play cards and talk about Shakespeare
with equal amounts of passion,
seated around our usual table in the corner.
Without fail, the staff at Rosie Lee's
knows we are coming.
They prepare extra plates
of rosemary chicken and wild rice.

Laughter springs in bursts from Samantha.
With smiling eyes,
she knows the strength and bend of my heart.
Pauline has languid, bawdy stories to weave—
I could sit and listen to her rich, round voice all night.
Sheila brings life and light everywhere she goes—
making me believe that we could jump
right through this roof,
if we wanted to.

We share a love of books—
the weight, texture, and scent of them.
We console each other over exam-time stress
and demanding professors.

Living inside the words,
the laughter,
and one too many pitchers of fruity wine,
exists the struggle to know ourselves fully.

Holding hands,
and our breath,
we take a great leap into the unknown
with a mighty yawp!

Disappearing Ghosts Dancing

inspired by Sunrise *by Mikalojus Konstantinas Čiurlionis*

My deep indigo dreams
bleed into morning,
permeate the ocean
of a new day.
Every ray of light
is a blessing and a prayer
for new beginnings.

Ghosts dance across the water
of placid glass,
characters leaping in mini memory clips,
the melding together of
every experience from yesterday—
the postman wishing me a good day,
my neighbor's dog wagging her joyful tail,
the owl in our backyard,
hooting her presence,
a watchful sentry perched on high.

The veil is lifted by a sunrise kiss,
warming the sea,
a golden-webbed touch,
a blueprint of possibility
imprinted on the surface.

Sunrise now lives inside my chest,
a thousand rays,
a thousand stories,
disappearing ghosts now dancing
within my quickening pulse.

Polished Pearl

I search for you,
plumb the depths of blue,
past the jagged, complex place
beneath the surface.
I keep looking, treading water,
until I let go of what can be seen,
until I feel my way through seaweed, dark matter,
to the strobe light of hope
living inside my lapis blue heart.
I loosen my grip, uncurl fingers,
expand my lungs in this underwater world,
discover that I was able to breathe all along.
I am the polished pearl held tightly in the shell.
I let go, reveal my curve, then shine.

Rx for Nourishment

Breathing in Tomorrow's Gold

The autumn sky is on fire with sun,
a riot of color fills the trees,
a Dali painting of dripping reds
and campfire orange.
The scent of burning leaves follows me,
as I walk into the quiet,
a new dimension of warm wind,
this new shift season.
My limbs feel lighter,
rabbits take cover under bushes,
and we hold stories close to our chests,
to the hearth of home.

When green turns to gold,
we go out into the world
in search of new beginnings.
If I kneel down by the stream of October,
my upturned palms anticipate, await.
I hear the echoes of past autumns,
schoolbooks and pumpkins,
soccer games and soaking up
the last rays of summer's fond glances.

Beginnings and endings melt together
in this time of golden days passing.
I harvest each memory,
images collected in a basket—
blankets on knees,
kettle corn in white paper bags,
sweaters with arms still too long,
thick slices of banana bread
with melting butter soaked in.

All things radiant sink into my veins,
the morning sun's breath causes fog
to float, then lift,
a magic trick,
this new day of wonder revealed,
this golden glory.

Every Moment

This is the sound a cup makes
when being filled.
This is the sound your heart makes
when pumping blood
to every other vein, organ,
and muscle in the body.
This is every cell singing its praises
to the moon of tomorrow.
This is your hand finding my hand
when we walk.
This is that swing you jumped off of
at the highest point
over stones in the playground.
This is your skin coming alive,
when the sun decided to
make this a day for
worshipping the soil.
This is every moment folding itself
into now.

The Gathering of Sustenance

inspired by Lunch Under the Canopy *by Claude Monet*

Light streams like ribbon on apple slices,
a pat of butter glistens on a baguette,
an outstretched hand offers both on a folded napkin.
We lean in closer,
share the intimacy of space and words
in between bites.
We gather up our lives,
offerings in spoonfuls,
cups brimming with details
of the everyday.
It is the sharing that sustains us.
The phone call from your son,
the postcard from my friend in Prague,
the walk we took by the water
this morning with the dog.

Our host unfolds a cloth
from an abundant basket,
revealing still warm banana bread.
He carefully places thick slices
on a blue, Chelsea patterned plate,
ensuring that every person
has a portion before taking one
for himself.
The canopy of shade frames
our gathering like a painting.
Our colors blend into one another,
a palette of afternoon sun
and sustenance.

Every Small Taste of Life

inspired by the poem "Praise" by Kelli Russell Agodon

The morning-rich joy of the perfect, runny egg
can make the sun sit on my chest,
as can the crunch of butter-drenched, multi-seed toast.
The way the morning air, still cool and crisp from night,
holds possibility,
like freshly showered, coconut-scented skin—
this is joy.
The day has not yet reached my pores.
I still hold the air of all of the hours
in my hopeful lungs.
Oh, how we fall in love with mist
rising from the grass,
spotting a doe and her fawn
emerging from the woods,
and the way light flirts with us
on the horizon of the lake.
The softness of afternoon speaks to me,
and evening's gentle touch beckons me
to lay down my burdens at the feet
of a welcoming couch,
a warm embrace,
the nourishing plate of grains,
meat, and vegetables.
But morning, morning allows me
to unselfconsciously delight
in every small taste of life,
every still lake at dawn
asking me to dwell in possibility.

The Gentle Holy

Hold words to your shoulders
like a sacred robe,
allow the fabric of love song
to caress the skin.
Feel the warmth, the weight,
the texture of empathy.

With the slip of silk,
kindness glides off the lips.
Clothe yourself in the gentle holy.
Welcome only this
into the sanctuary of your life.

Slow Motion Peace

With papers flying off the counter,
the room buzzing and humming
with a busy pulse,
my fingers don't know what
to do with my pen.
The microwave dings,
it calls me to stop,
halt.

I see plumes of smoke,
from my too fast brain
and my too fast feet,
start to dissipate in the air.
Slow motion takes over.

My hand pulls the sliding glass door open.
Summer is a cicada's ring,
announcing the blazing heat,
the lazy sound of suspension.
These are the days
I wish I had a hammock.
A doe and her fawn pause
by the shade of a tree,
holding my gaze,
all three of us motionless,
drinking in the quiet,
allowing muscles to practice
knitting back together.
Instead of leaping into the woods,
they stroll towards the pond,
nudging the tall grass with their noses,
nudging me closer and closer
to a thing resembling peace.

Sacred Pause

The steady drumbeat of water
leads my limbs in a salsa dance,
hot steam mixing
with the scent of lemon verbena, patchouli.
Triple milled soap suds glide
and coat my shoulders,
swirling circles of clean.
I raise my chin, breathe in
the sacred, holy moments of pause.
Sometimes, I place my hands over my heart,
slow my movements to slow my pulse,
feel the intensity of heat pinking my skin.
I wash off yesterday,
allow pores to open,
welcoming the new story of now
with an open, heart chakra glow.
I dance with my clean outline,
feel the floor beneath me,
in sync with shower rhythm, waterfall flow,
footsteps walking towards
some unknown destination,
some not yet known celebration
of an undiscovered me.

Catching Feathers

inspired by The Victory *by René Magritte*

The soul should stand ajar, says Dickinson,
so I stand at the doorway of joy,
where land meets sea,
the waves of life's small, crashing moments
licking my feet with salt,
ushering me into the next breath
and then, the next.

I sit further up on the beach,
contemplate the clouds,
their pillow softness,
and imagine every sun-filled memory
I can touch—
the quiet exhale of my first-born son
after nursing,
when his head rested on my shoulder,
his tiny form, barely reaching my waist.

Another cloud passes by.
I get lost in the opaque white,
think of the waterfall in Ambleside
where we took that family photo,
mist coating our faces as we smiled
for the camera.

I look deeper into
the blue expanse of ocean,
see my father eating a bowl
of clam chowder in the pub in Newport,
called The Black Pearl,
how happy this made him,
this simple pairing of black pepper,
clams, and cream.

I leave my soul ajar
so that joy may find a way in,
like mist,
like memory,
like life dropping a feather
from the clear blue sky.

What I Packed for You

We place and stack your new, shiny things
for the dorm in our car.
The clear boxes hold
instant oatmeal and crackers,
because I won't be there
to make you things late at night.
They hold extra shampoo and tissues,
in case you run out of essentials.
They hold a soft robe and new socks,
because this is how my love is translated—
into things you will wear.

Mixed in with the notebooks and highlighters
are stamps and envelopes
for the letters we hope you might write to us,
hooks to hang your favorite poster of wildflowers,
a First Aid kit, because I won't be there
to hand you a Band-Aid
or bring you Advil.

Away from home, I will still be with you.
In these clear, overstuffed boxes,
somehow my hands will appear.
You will see what I touched
and touch the love tucked inside,
holding you—still.

Newfound Lungs

a letter to my sons

Every day is an algebraic equation,
too many variables to keep track of.
We are swirling energy,
silver comets destined
to land or travel aimlessly.

Ground yourself in red jasper soil.
Plunge eager hands into salt water.
Find the lifeline of earth,
the running thread of equator
hot lava breath,
the fire of now,
the life pulse of who you are today.

Tomorrow will appear in its own time,
a feathered guest
whispering verbs
you are not yet ready to hear.

Your borrowed tongue
paints words on paper,
wisdom from your aging bones.

Littering the sky is every sound uttered,
every heart song you belt out
with newfound lungs.

Rest Here in My Chest

The narrow, bumpy path
became a tunnel of joy at twilight.
Slowly, we approached a hidden shoreline.

Our evening picnic mission
was shared by other sunset revelers,
a perfect, peach moment.
Rumpled blankets, baskets holding
carefully cut sandwiches
and bottles of champagne appeared,
dotting the sand like small villages.

Orange-pink hues floated down, drifting,
resting in swaths of silk in the sky.
Each minute that passed
caused colors to deepen
and bloom above our heads.

We took countless photos as a family,
and then, just of our sons.
Never again would they be 18 and 16.

This moment was too delicious.
Don't leave, I thought.
Stay golden—
rest here in my chest.

Infinite and Holy

I am teaching myself
how to live again,
how to transform my giving heart
into a resilient one,
one that I take care of—
honor the presence of.

I dance in this circle of love,
the center of source
and all that is.
I want to exist here,
not just keep the embers warm,
the routines and patterns ingrained,
the clockwork of chores.

A courageous trust in living
walks into the room, like a lion,
takes me by the hand,
walks me up the volcano's mount
to where my ancestors now stand,
and I see the horizon for what it is—
infinite and holy.

Marbled Glory, a Meditation

inspired by the sculpture Breathing Dance *by Elza Kövesházi-Kalmár*

Every breath is a meditation,
a steadfast trust in moving from
moment to moment.
Lift your gaze, your chin,
move the tender palms of your hands
upwards,
as if gently holding
the weight of all things.
Let there be a string of energy from the body
to the sky, so that the blue above infuses
skin, veins, and feet.
The space between hands and hips
becomes filled with temporary wings,
reminding you that you are not earthbound.
The mind becomes air,
becomes the gentle blanket around shoulders,
becomes the resting place for body
and all things bountiful.
We are marbled glory,
traveling across oceans
without moving an inch.

Double Helix Hope

Fingers touch fresh raindrops
on a leaf,
and I imagine other hands in a circle
feeling the same sensation of water—
fluid movement of droplets
across skin.

I travel the world
on foot, by train, by boat.
On each journey
I meet a person
who offers me a peach
or a wedge of bread.
We exchange smiles,
look deeply into each other's eyes,
and for that split second,
we become the same person—
a double helix flow
of perpetual energy that compels us
to move together as one.
We are each other's hope.

Rx for Healing

A Painted Kiss

My lips are confetti,
a celebration of whispers,
painted words emerging,
heart songs,
secret colors,
thoughts escaping
from this liquid heart.

I feel like a raw nerve,
an open wound,
a walking emotion with bare feet.
I feel every scratch,
every abrasion.

Sometimes there is no protection.
We cannot take cover,
avoid the jagged rocks of transition.

Embrace the torn wing,
that limp you nurse.
I offer you this painted kiss,
a speckled, healing gift.

In Search of Tiny Forest Gods

A sharp stitch of pain in my abdomen
throws sparks of electricity
throughout my once lithe body,
a memento from surgery.
And yet, I continue to follow
the well-worn path of the mountain.
A trickle of water escapes
from the lake, at the very top.
A wild, zig-zag pattern of water falling
becomes my focal point,
a healing gaze,
the anticipated happiness
that keeps my feet moving.

I pause, kneel at the altar of nature to pray,
an exercise in gratitude,
a reason to sit, take a pill for inflammation,
breathe in the apparitions of tiny forest gods
floating in my field of vision.

We carry on after sharing baguettes
with tuna, mayo, and poppyseeds.
A flood of ramblers pass us, going up,
and then another stream hikes down with purpose.
To be at peace with myself
is to accept that halfway up the mountain
is enough.
This day, this moment of trying, is enough.
I am enough.

Sound Healing

It begins with silent footsteps
in the woods,
the first few drops from the sky
filtering through branches and leaves,
whispered stories of the earth
told over and over.

A heavier downpour appears,
the soil drinks a tall glass,
replenished.
The world is now an orchestra
of green sound and healing,
supporting our breath,
our feet,
our new vine growth,
our rooted connection—
a lighted lamp for all who seek.

Rain Museum

The silver promise
of rain appears,
and we hear the applause
of leaves,
a percussive music.

We watch water gather
on the table outside,
a museum of joy
where we have summer suppers,
witness turkeys marching
across the lawn,
sip iced tea and read books.
The air lifts,
wings of reflected light,
raindrops floating,
effortlessly letting go.

The clouds have been holding onto hope.
Abundance now falls
and covers the world
with possibility.
We welcome tomorrow,
walk outside to know ourselves,
let our faces get wet.

Where Tender Truth Sings

There is an opening at the heart,
a key hole at the chest's center
where every, tender truth sings,
where brave words live,
a lower layer of music, like pulse,
where many-colored petals and feathers
spill out and flutter,
changing the air's vibration.
The heart is a tuning fork
for what our lips tremble to speak of
and find a humming harmony for.
This is where the greening grass grows,
where birds hover and float,
where our truest selves leap
through boundaries, now untethered,
fly free
to the tallest treetops,
sit perched on the horizon of being
and breathe.

These Things We Hold

My lower back aches from the bag I am carrying.
It holds the phone call I missed from our son,
feeling unprepared for a class I was teaching,
and the look of disappointment,
imagining I had let people down.
It holds my fear of losing loved ones, one by one,
as though my arms won't have as much to embrace.

When I sit and unpack the bag,
allow the things that I call things
to fall to the ground,
evaporate in the morning air,
I see that tucked inside,
are perfectly folded squares
of what I love.

I see the delicious image
of my youngest son's bare feet
tickled by a bed of dew-kissed grass,
his impish smile, his earnest eyes
that search mine and light me up from inside.
I taste the first spoonful of ice cream,
then offer up a bite to my husband,
as he prepares to feed me a dollop of his.
I feel the beautiful, bone-crushing closeness
of my oldest son's 20-second hugs,
the ones that fill my lungs with
every ounce of oxygen I could possibly need.

My shoulders carry both the weight
and weightlessness of this life.
My bag keeps emptying and filling.
I let go of it all,
let my heart take photographs of today.

How to Stay Grounded in Times of Flux

Do not cling to clouds,
but rather notice the billowing outlines.
Notice the shades of opal-like white
morphing into hues of heather gray
or charcoal, misty smoke.
See the blue behind the sky's pillows
and know that this promise exists for you, too.

When the snow melts to rivulets
on the sidewalk,
and the earth thaws
to a softening green bed,
be barefoot in the yard,
let roots reach beneath your feet
to the very center of soil.
Let the trees know you are listening.

Walk in the sun as much as you can,
so that your hair is light-soaked
and your cheeks are kissed
by rays of canary yellow.
Just the movement of following
the sun's progress
connects you to every other living thing
seeking oxygen,
a community of breath.

Green yourself like a leaf,
drinking in droplets of water,
slowing yourself down to the minute pace of growth.
Your stillness becomes
part of the landscape,

so that even the wind thinks
you are tied to the earth
by invisible strings,
inextricably connected
by a force greater than human ambition.
You have left that nonsense behind
in favor of branches and birdsong.
When a storm comes,
you are grounded.

When You Hear Ada Limón Read a Poem

with a last line by Ada Limón

You are hearing the heart of someone
who knows life from the cells out,
from the outside of her skin, in.

You are hearing her warmth,
her nourishing smile,
her love for every connected muscle and bone.
You are hearing words cascade
effortlessly from Light source,
from a powerhouse of energy
that shows us how love can surge,
how words can heal,
and how our humanity
is something to be honored,
held in a deep well of reverence.

She is housing tomorrow
in carefully chosen lines
that will lead us to a new day,
that will lead us to ourselves
in ways we did not know we could see,
did not know how to see,
until Ada unveiled for us
the gold that lives in our veins
and flows, endlessly.
We are source, too, she tells us,
. . . and your bones are my bones
and isn't that enough?

The Stillness of Enough

We knit ourselves together
with small acts of love,
quiet moments of stillness.

Rows and rows of loops
held together by patience
become a counting meditation,
as I weave a blended mix
of nylon and wool yarn.
Each multi-colored stitch of
under, around, under, and through
becomes a prayer—
my prayer for today,
to pass time with more peace.
I look down at the soft, patterned road
of fabric I have crafted
and beam at how it now resembles a scarf.
Inch by inch,
row by row,
it is starting to become something.

I, too, am becoming,
without rushing,
without a Singer machine motor,
just these imperfect hands—
lovingly creating something.
This is the only purpose I need.

A Thousand Notes with Wings

Release the pain body
housed in small cells.
The sharp knife cuts
of memory
no longer serve you.
Tomorrow's knitted muscles
dwell in strong canyons,
the alcoves where
that dancing self
longs to spin,
like the vinyl record
playing Thumbelina all day.
She knows where joy lives.
A thousand notes with wings
all fly from your chest now.
Each orange-black fluttering
lets go.

White Light and Lava

I am wearing my coat of colors today,
even though there is no wind,
and the air is mild.
Everything I touch comes to life,
so I keep warm with softened cloth,
despite the ready sun.

I enfold myself with imaginary wings,
shelter the heart from storms—
the energy that flies out of mouths,
like white light and lava.
If only I could hold up a shield,
carry an umbrella to catch what falls,
prevent my hair from getting wet.

Beads of water appear
on my hands, feet, lips.
I collect them in open palms,
offer them up to the soil,
a gift of other people's tears.
I hum the sound of healing,
let the notes linger.

A Salve

A salve made from hemp,
a broth made from bone.

I can't remember which surgery this was for,
but Karen brought me her homemade bone broth.
You need this, she said.
A lovingly wrapped container
appeared on my porch within hours.
Also, a small, silver disk
containing a hemp-based salve
to soothe my aching back.
It will help with sleep, she said.

I hadn't seen Karen in months,
but when she heard I was recovering,
she went into action—
an angel at my doorstep,
a nurse with light footsteps.

There are times when we know
we are touched by something higher,
a realm where all of our needs are met,
where our hearts are held
like the delicate, fragile, flowering shapes they are,
where our hands touch an invisible cord of light
and we are healed.

Rx for Raising Humans

When Our Son Became a Magpie

When did you first lose your son? I think.
Nothing tragic, no need for weeping.
And yet, I grieve
for all of the small, unobserved ways
in which our oldest has left our nest
threadbare, lacking fresh straw.
Our weathered hearts
just a bit fragile,
as we notice less abundance,
fewer chicks chirping for our attention.

This is the natural order of things.
He is meant to collect shiny things,
like a magpie,
delight us with his new world,
tinsel and stardust adventures,
send up smoke in the air
then disappear,
like the true magician that he is.

Blink and you'll miss it—
the years he was here,
and then the brief hours
when he rests in one spot to share his life,
over a meal or a cup of tea.

My husband and I scurry
around the kitchen,
bring him his favorite treats.
His brother asks his opinion on a song he is writing.

We gather up our longing for connection
in the fabric of our family's blanket,
take turns feeling its softness,
then one by one,
we let go,
new colors appearing.
Blue and red stripes
becoming an unexpected, solid purple.

On the Edge of Next

I sing into the cathedral of this day,
the sacred gift of now
speaking from my lungs,
a deep knowing, a spacious presence.
On the sidewalk,
a single dandelion reaches up,
proof that life keeps going,
we all keep growing,
whether consciously, or not.

The summer air is a lullaby,
a thread of comfort
at the season's end.
On the edge of next,
our family huddles,
sharing time,
holding the handles of a few hours
in a circle of the familiar.
We sip coffee, read books, check phones,
but we do these simple things together,
hold the container of our unit of four,
before the shape changes.

We are a rocking boat
carried closer to shore.
Someone tracks the wind,
someone keeps the balance by sitting,
someone keeps an eye out for land,
and we all watch the water in awe—
at how it keeps moving.

Seeing Your Own Gold

For the fragile way you look in the mirror,
I want you to see the beautiful arch of your brows,
the way autumn's breeze tussles your hair
when we walk.
I want you to love every inch of your skin
and live in it more,
dance more freely,
with those willow branch limbs,
step into the light
and own the space where you stand.

When the sun comes up every morning,
I want you to see your own glory,
the way you see the wonder
of shimmering wheat fields
and billowing clouds,
when you paint.
I want you to see your own gold.

When we sit to eat dinner
and you thank me
for a bowl of swirled pasta with parmesan,
I want you to see the true thankfulness
shining in my eyes—
my gratitude for you,
the presence you encompass,
and the rounded wholeness
the world now has
because you are in it.

The Cloak of Memory

I remember mist falling
when we walked,
how the world greeted us
with a welcoming green,
a layer of hope,
a cloak of forgiveness
for our imperfect, human selves.

I wrap myself in this cloak today,
feeling every emotion,
as we prepare to take our son to college,
forgiving myself for easy tears.

If time machines existed,
I would return to our family hike
in The Lake District,
stand at the waterfall a moment longer,
linger over scones with clotted cream.
I would patiently watch the newborn sheep
struggle to stand,
marveling at how the mother would nudge
her baby forward in the field,
watchful but confident
in her offspring's ability to walk.

The mist reminds me that
more rain is coming,
that we can weather any storm.
Memory houses us,
keeps us dry.

Inviting New Songs

Just three days before your move,
I could think of nothing else—
the huddled crowd of bags and bins
in our sitting room,
the way your bedroom was gaining space,
like a mouth losing teeth,
the labels and reminder notes
on anything that wasn't moving,
the way my eyes would swell
with tears, in anticipation of your leaving.

This is good. This is what happens next.
I gave myself pep talks
to ease the transition.

In the midst of preparations,
we rehearsed for an open mic.
All of us ignored the word, *college*.
I held a sheet of paper with lyrics,
sang my favorite Sarah Harmer song
with your father,
listened to you and your brother strum guitars,
performing with gusto and smiling friends.

This is good, I thought. This is what happens next.
A month after moving you into the dorm,
the house will feel less empty,
your phone calls and texts will be
events of happiness,
but we will also prepare to sing again.
We will hold a microphone,
send melodies into the air
with a newfound confidence,

reclaim an old passion,
thankful for the letting go
that led to inviting these new notes.

We Carry Tiny Planets of Love

Each moment, a perfect pearl,
a galaxy,
a beautiful mystery.
We collect stars in wine glasses,
as if we could sip the universe,
as if we could contain it.

The map of life, like constellations,
sends little flickers into the night air,
embers of days.
Not wanting to drop a single memory,
carrying them in my arms,
holding them close to my chest,
I make a sacred record, as if sculpted in earth—
the way you bounced to the music,
pointing to the play button
again and again,
the way your big brother pronounced turtle
as *tuttle,*
the way you both sat together at a tiny, wooden table
with chairs shaped like elephants,
the photo of both of you on the leather chair,
holding a hula hoop like a frame,
smiling at me through the years
in a time machine on paper.

I marvel at the sky,
at how my love for two sons
revolves around them,
like planets, like a weather system,
like the many, wondrous, ordinary days
that keep collecting and disappearing.
My arms try to carry them all,
tiny, glowing spheres reaching skyward.

Tashmoo Beach Smiles

We stand on rocks,
take selfies with the sunset,
our beaming smiles
filling the rectangular screen of your phone.
This is what swallowing a peach must feel like,
soothing oranges and yellows
smoothing the skin,
a satiated belly
jumping with laughter.
We bat away the mosquitos,
trying to outrun them,
refusing to leave the beach,
despite the night descending,
urging our departure.
My toes find joy in the sand,
my calves relish the deep massage
of cascading waves.
I watch our two sons pose and wave,
take one last photo with my eyes,
before we pile into the car.
Sand follows us, clings to our shoes,
not wanting us to leave either.
We hold the moment just a touch longer,
watch the peach leave our skin,
returning to sky.

Winged Secrets in the Chest

inspired by an image by Yasin Aribuga

Stand still,
hold your hand out,
be patient.

Our youngest son,
eyes wide to any shift in the air,
any changes felt on the skin,
remained statue-like, poised,
ready to receive.

We stood in line for entry,
a hot house room with windows on the ceiling
and wings on every leaf.
This was the art of waiting—
the trickle of sweat
as we melted
in the indoor rain forest.

While other children cupped their hands,
reaching out into the space
of not yet appearing flight,
both of our sons gently looked
with gold-touched eyes of awe,
respect for habitat.
Never assuming they should possess,
they witnessed,
leaving this world untouched,
observing with the heart,
taking mental photographs
to transform into harmonic chords on the guitar
or the graceful shapes of a sketch.

Looking back across winged time,
I see how the monarch's stained-glass stripes
informed my younger son's brushstrokes,
how the two-tailed swallowtail taught his brother
to layer background vocals over
a subtle piano line.
The secrets of the butterfly room
cannot be taken,
they must be felt inside the chest.

Sifting

I sift days through my fingers,
like green blades of grass caressing skin,
breathe in the last open moments of summer.
The oven of high noon
cools quickly now,
even before dusk,
reminding me that September
will require warm fabric on my shoulders.
Winter is the dream at my feet,
I am not yet able to see.
For now, I will bask in the tender
passing of fading light,
the time we have left before studies
and textbooks are gathered up,
before footsteps leave early
and arrive late,
before root vegetables fall into stew,
before I hold the memory close to my chest
of sharing frozen custard with my son,
before his driving lessons turn into solo trips,
and I am waving to him from the front door.

Where My Curved Arms Arch

for my nieces

This body once housed
the budding leaves of two sons.
Sometimes they still walk where my footsteps
leave imprints,
they still nestle in the space
where my curved arms arch—
wide open parentheses.
There is room for more.
I have ample space in this heart.
For the daughters who never
joined me on earth,
I know now that they were simply
bowing their heads,
in prayer and in wait,
knowing that my ventricled rooms
needed more chairs for you—
my nieces who now need
extra cushions of love.

These hands knit and bead
with dedicated string.
I offer you my words,
threading stories and comfort
with woven care.
I offer you my heart
that listens and picks up the phone
on the first ring.
I offer you these things,
because my mothering heart source
is a boundless field you can count on
and come to.

You can run to me.
I will be here—
the open arms of aunt,
the heart of mothered love.

Time Traveling with Planets

We are connected by invisible wires,
transporting light beams,
words, slowed breathing,
my love for you.

Your hurried goodbye on a Monday
escapes your lips
in the darkness of winter's dawn.
I exhale sleep,
that liminal state just before the world
brings me into day's light.

Our sons still dream on creased pillows.
The house creaks and moans
as the heat bellows through the vents.
Every ghost of every day before this one
filters through,
a silvery flow,
a thin streak of otherworldly vapor.

On my own, with the task
of stirring young children,
moving pots around on the stove,
refilling the cat's bowl with kibble,
I, too, move as slowly
as the planets,
not quite in the groove.

Monday becomes Friday.
Your plane lands in the evening.
The week lays its soft head
on my lap.

You walk through the door,
a world weary traveler.
Tiny footsteps rush to the door.
Little hands reach out for your pockets,
tug at the fabric of your coat,
imagining the you from Monday
and breathing in the sun of your arrival
from some distant star.

Rx for Grief Work

Sacred Stones of Loss

I distract myself,
counting the number of circles
in the room—
coffee mug rims,
a ceiling fan spinning,
tarnished brass doorknobs,
a mirror in the hallway.
I exist within
the white space of absence.
There is comfort in shapes.

Overlapping circles of memory
stack themselves
into a tower of different
decades, geographies,
individual moments
with my father.
I see the glass fish tank from the 70's
and the smaller globe of guppies beside it.
We spent hours watching life swim in lazy circles.
I see the foreign landscape of haybales
when we moved from New York.
The air was fresh and quiet,
a gust of wind replacing honking horns.
I remember you picking up a gingko leaf
and saving it for my science project.
Evening walks became a quest
for new plant species.

Each memory is now a small, sacred stone.
I hold the roundness,
my upturned palms in prayer,
giving thanks
for what remains.

A River of Blessings

follows me,
as I walk in remembrance,
recall the lexicon of grief
that was my companion
before, during, and in the
months after my father's funeral.
Missing the notes of his laughter,
hearing his stories,
knowing that his energy lives on
in our words,
every time we mention our world
with him in it.
With autumn comes the pause
before winter,
before cocooning,
when I can easily stop time,
recall our walks with the dog,
the crunching of leaves beneath our feet,
our sacred bond of appreciation
for the deep, mimosa color of dying leaves,
how the world at this time
starts to close its windows.
Its wings are folded over
like a dove shielding its young.
How I long for and want
to be shielded again,
you holding an umbrella over us both,
not caring if you get wet,
making me feel dry,
even if my feet are now drenched
with memory.

The Salt That Remains

It lasts longer than braided leather.
It endures beyond the lifespan
of the oldest oak—
the way our broken, human selves connect
and live on in one another.

From one moment to the next,
we pass the baton of memory.
We seek the seed.
We go back to the beginning.
We hold sacred each and every word,
like pearls in the palm,
like notes on the piano,
floating and finding a home
in the hope chest of the heart.

Long after the wood on the house
becomes weathered
and the driveway needs repaving,
I will remember the way you
sanded a single plank after cutting it down
to size, just so the deck would be sturdy.

Long after the pretzels are gone
from the bag,
and the salt blows away in the wind,
I will remember the way your laughter
became high-pitched
in between telling colorful jokes—
punctuated by salty bites.

Long after the netting has frayed
and the white lines need to be repainted,
again and again,
I will remember you teaching my
insecure, 13-year-old self
how to throw a basketball
before gym class the next day.

Long after my oldest is off at college,
and the Baldwin piano goes silent,
I will remember hearing your bold chords
from the old living room in New Jersey.

Long after wood becomes dust,
long after stone becomes rubble,
my memories of you remain
in the outline of every setting sun.

Stepping into the Greening Moments

Walking with loss
in a new way today,
as if finding forgotten, rugged shoes
in the back of the closet
meant for longer hikes in spring.
I celebrate small pebbles of memory,
reassured by the weight of a speckled-brown agate
or the clear, crystalized light of a citrine.

Rather than leave them in a jar
or on a dresser,
I carry the stones with me,
so that your eyes see what I see.
You are not missing these sun-dappled moments.
You are enjoying them with us,
sharing in the colors of every mellow, peach sunset
and every whispered, honey dawn.

In my mind, you notice the little girl
with bouncing curls,
waiting with her mother in line.
You notice the small dog on my walk
with happy, shining eyes.
So I stop the way you would stop,
bend down to greet this undeniable burst of life.

This is how I will let go of loss,
by carrying you with me,
with each step into new moments,
accumulating like so many greening leaves.

The Space My Father Filled

inspired by The Listening Room *by René Magritte*

Your memory fills space,
expands to fill the whole room,
any room,
like a gargantuan piece of ripe fruit.
I cannot possibly see or hear all of it
in one sitting.
Furniture bursts through windows,
like a tree that will not stop growing.
The sound of your shoes is an echo.
I picture your train collection,
rows and rows,
neatly displayed small villages of motion.

I want to remember
and I don't want to remember.
Breakfast still needs to be made,
bills paid, laundry folded.
But sometimes, I sit with the giant apple
and ponder the shape of you,
the way you read the same articles,
forgetting them,
wanting to share them with us.
I remember the sound of no sound,
when you listened and smiled,
folded your hands on the table
as if in prayerful attention to my life,
joy sparking light in your eyes.

Your Story Sings Through Me

Your memories
and my memories of you
run deep,
like the rippled reflections of orange-red
in a koi pond,
the inviting mystery,
the plunging depth of color.

I thought you took your stories with you
when departing this world,
but then reels of film kept appearing,
a night-time movie in my dreams,
a daily ritual of time travel,
when days and years flooded brain cells,
an excavation of family history,
like the paintings of your Uncle Jules
that I had never seen,
but somehow knew in my veins,
the texture of oils on canvas.

I am the hoop dancer at the water's edge,
a flash of spinning red.
I am yesterday, today, and tomorrow.
I am the imprint of your life well-lived,
now singing through my DNA,
the spark of life in your grandsons.
Even blinded by the cloth of earthly existence,
I still see you.
I can see for centuries.

When Sorrow Is Untidy

after Lucille Clifton

Dear Sorrow,

I hear your tears gather,
lapping up against the shore.
There is seaweed and debris here,
emotions you left untidy,
in need of mending,
in need of something.
You know not yet how to heal.

I will house your pain,
hold your hands,
shelter you from yourself.
Every cup in the cupboard
is a place for you to fill
and be filled.
Come rest here,
come unfold yourself,
come let the weight of the day
drop, fall, dwell.
Together we can find our way
out of the forest.
First, we will listen to the music of trees.

Open Your Eyes

with a first line by Galway Kinnell

Wait, for now.
Wait for the storm to pass over,
to tunnel through the sky
like an angry tornado.
Grief, apathy, sadness—
the ache of loss
and the trembling for
all that we think will crumble,
will not leave our world for long.

The soft pillow of hope will return,
like a cloud in the shape of two hands
holding a dove.
The wind that moves a stray hair
out of your eyes
will also return.
The moon, Jupiter,
the little dipper,
your hesitant smile,
these things will all return.

Please—
please wait, for now.
You will see yourself reach,
green, and flower.
You will see yourself
eat a big bowl of pasta with
enjoyment and abandon,
a small collection of Parmesan flakes
on your shirt.
You will return to yourself
as if you had never left,
the calm after the storm,
opening your eyes once again.

When We Open the Next Door

for William Norcross

We were swimming underwater,
the film from seaweed already
compromising sight,
when we heard the news
that you were gone.
Your once strong, beating heart
now silent.

We were looking in the rearview mirror,
ignoring the horizon.
You quietly slipped away,
inside time's envelope.

Our rushed flurry through life
abruptly stopped.
The lights now seem dimmer
with you gone.
We are swimming in
even murkier waters.

Our once asleep selves
awakened.
This is what happens
in the dawn of grief.
Our pulse quickens,
then slows to molasses.
Our eyes burn
from the brightness of loss,
the sharp pang
of presence ripped
from our tongues.

In place of oxygen,
there are roots growing—
the echo of your chuckle,
the way your nose would wrinkle
and your eyes would squint,
when telling a raunchy joke,
that Matthew Sweet song you played
endlessly during showers.

Memories lengthen,
like the wide-open arms of your Nana
waiting to greet you.

The song, *Entreat Me Not to Leave Thee,*
sings in my head.
This is a temporary goodbye,
until we hear your guitar playing
for each of us,
when we open the next door.

Capturing Light

for my father

Departure—sudden leaving, like early thaw, like low tide time
Looked for light, letters in drawers, lost messages, whispers in
    dreams
Your echo is a lightning bug, my memory is the jar.

Things That Float from One Realm to the Next

for Will

Before you left,
the twinkle lights
danced in the garage,
when we closed our eyes.
We could hear the suitcase drum kit
beating on its own,
like your big heart drumming.

Before you left,
the air felt easier to breathe,
our laughter
quick, like pulse.
Now, we pause
before letting sound escape our lips.
We walk more slowly from room to room,
as if expecting the shadow and sun of your smile
to be around every corner.

So I place a photo of you and your girls
on the bench in our sitting room.
I leave my announcement post,
with huddled family images, pinned,
because you are still here,
offering someone another drink,
offering your own chair,
so that someone else can sit,
offering up your song
for eager ears,
offering up the watch on your wrist
to our oldest son,
offering up one of your guitars
to our youngest.

He now joins the ranks
of Norcross men who
conjure magic with strings and frets,
who fashion myth and legend
out of whispered words
that float from one realm
to the next.

A Shared Rest

Grief has no expiry date.
There is no right or wrong way
to walk this path.
It is a winding road
with pitfalls and footfalls,
grassy outposts,
and weary, fellow travelers.

Some days,
we carry loss, gently, in cupped hands.
Other days,
it carries us
on curved, but sturdy shoulders,
when we need the weight lifted.

Within the misty spaces,
the tucked away
mole moments of time,
when the outer world's hasty pace
no longer calls to us,
when only the quiet needs
of the body beckon,
we can sit side by side
with grief,
offer it milky tea and biscuits,
share a bench seat together in the woods
and rest.

Everything Becomes Again

Everything becomes undone—
the dishes in the cupboard,
the neatly folded laundry,
the tidiness of tomorrow's plans.

Everything you've carefully put away
will end up in a tangled mess
on the living room floor—
those muddied boots,
your pale pink humility,
your rash of grief,
your vulnerable, weary self.

Everything will catch up with you—
that late night of screen time,
those white, powdered donuts,
that trip you always meant to take,
those words you swallowed whole,
that neglected ulcer.

Everything will be OK, I promise—
the lack you carry in a black velvet pouch,
the hurt you wear, like a tattoo sleeve,
the ache you cannot fill with earth.

Everything becomes again—
the hope-filled you from 1995,
the green of the backyard
where the snapping turtle strolls,
the new leaf you
still stretching in the soil.
Everything, everything becomes again.

A Twilight Glimpse

Folding the laundry
is usually the chore I avoid,
bags of clean fabric
waiting to be put into neat piles.
On days when my mind drifts to loss,
I turn on peaceful music,
without lyrics or percussion.
I allow myself to become part
of the movement,
the repeated routine
of folding things over and over.
I forget the task,
ponder how long it has been
since I've seen someone.
I drift off through the window,
wandering on the moor,
into the clouds beyond.

When my hands come back into focus,
the room has changed color,
from yellowed daylight to lavender dusk.
My skin now has more lines.
I have aged a lifetime
and a day.
I can see clear beyond,
through the walls
and into the next life
that waits for us,
the next level of twilight knowing,
only glimpsed at
when we blink.

Coming Up Roses

for Tara

The sky is weeping rain,
because you are not here.
Your voice appears,
you say my name.
You tell me, *It's OK, Cristina. I'm OK.*
I see your dimples
in the photo I now keep
tucked into my mirror.
I imagine your smile,
your black pearl eyes.

As Dainty June,
you could do a triple pirouette
without a drop of sweat,
leap through the air
like a gazelle,
furred pinstripes, a blur in the air.

I had a dream
that everything was coming up roses.
We were stretching backstage,
our arched feet reaching
for tomorrow with such eagerness.

A white butterfly now visits me
on the front porch,
as I listen to the duet
we used to sing.
It weaves in and out of the bushes,
effortlessly free,
just as you are
now.

Rx for Inspiration

Hay Bale Awakenings

An empty field transformed
became an oil painting
framed by golden light
and the halo of dawn.
The walk I had taken every day
bloomed into something new.
Giant, concentric circles of calm appeared
just past the wooden fence
where sheep used to graze
and horses once stood by trees.
The hay bales called to me
as if singing the day into existence,
a chorus of wheat angels beckoning the morning,
teasing us all into an awakening
of limbs now moving with grace,
minds now open to every new flicker of thought
sprouting through soil.
These are ancient beings,
unmoved, unruffled,
mountains showing us the way,
with the patient steadfastness
of mother love.

Dancing

What I remember most about being a dancer
is not my pinched toes against a semi-circle of wool,
sweat-drenched cotton tights,
or the relentless, 3-hour rehearsals.
What my body retains, memorized by cells, by neurons,
is that indescribable moment of blissful spin,
lifted suspension in the air,
the balanced arabesque on pointe,
that nanosecond of experiencing effortlessness.
I remember the feeling of arms, legs,
arched feet, even my chin, all working together,
finding that impossible to define
space and moment when time stops,
flows through my fingertips, lengthening the spine.
Weightless, my dancer's spirit keeps going
where limbs leave off
and the world somehow feels lighter,
piano music in sync
with blood flow and breath.
When the next leap begins,
the next pirouette, the next grand jeté,
muscle memory takes over—
the room dances me into another existence.

With Stones in Her Mouth

An aging rose,
a crone
with stones in her mouth,
she follows me from across the room
and chuckles.
Thin-lipped with browning petals,
the wise woman
begs me to pause and look
at my own reflection.
How fleeting this all is, she says,
how miraculous.
A velvet softness,
a land of forgetting
that beckons us to awaken.
You hold sunlit gold in your palms,
wear the lines of presence
on the soles of your feet.
Light bearer, seeker—
write me down,
let me breathe in the liminal spaces,
let me live through your words
and lyrics.
Let me dance in your hair.

To Greet Each Moment with Awakening

Sometimes the moon
sits on my chest,
and I hold the unbearable
weight of light,
only to discover
that I am light, too—
gold-touched fingertips,
dancing feet
waiting at the top of a mountain—
to be reached,
to be loved,
for every sparkling cell
to sing.

I Rise to Meet Her Wings

Sometimes a new life
is the tall grass
obscuring the edge of the pond,
or leaving for another country—
your cells replaced by
the sound of sheep in the morning
and stone walls with history
growing through the vines and cracks.

I imagine roots traveling and spiraling
beneath my feet, into the soil.
I look up at dusk to find
cotton candy pink and teal blue swirls in the sky,
a surround sound expanse of color.
My oldest son and I stand
in the center of this circle,
listening to the close of one day
and the whispered entrance of the next.

My spine begins to lengthen again.
I stand beneath the tree in our front yard,
beckoned by the thin, high voice
of a rose-breasted grosbeak.
We look at each other—
I rise to meet her wings.

Chocolate Chips Straight from the Bag

Joy called me back to my feet
after many months of not dancing.
She walked right up to me
and gave me a pinch.
No gentle nudges this time.
It was a bite on the bum,
forcing me to see the white cottontail
of a rabbit jump out of our bushes
and run spiritedly into the woods.
Joy would not stand for my quiet,
the body being lodged.
She encouraged me to belly dance in the kitchen,
create a makeshift bird feeder out of old pantyhose,
and eat chocolate chips straight from the bag.

Gold Dust

I walk under the tree branch,
allow leaves to smoothly brush
the top of my head.
A pool of sunlight appears,
the golden nest bed
where cottonwood blossoms rest their eyes.

I drop bruised apples at the edge of the forest,
knowing that rabbits, turkeys, deer,
and one shy raccoon will feast on last week's fruit.

In the shade of tall trees,
I pause, look past our backyard
into the clearing,
where the hidden lake lives,
where my dreams for tomorrow
lie just beyond,
where the me of 30 years ago
still lives in the hive of my consciousness.

I see her,
that young woman
with the dangling carnelian earrings,
who spent hours at Octopus Books
reading about Frida Kahlo
and sipping a single coffee all afternoon.

I was born to dance in pools of light.
I am made of air,
transparent wings,
and that fine dust of gold
that appears for just one hour each day.

To Uncurl Roots

Lightning crashes,
the energy of elders awakens.
Lines on my face grow deeper.
I feel jagged cracks in time,
breaks in the pavement,
the spiny veins of leaves.

Listening, breathing,
closing my eyes to the inauthentic,
they tell me to let go,
to let the mighty rivers flow,
to uncurl my rooted toes.
But I hold on—
for you.

The song of ancients
resides in me.
I birth the universe—
an upheaval,
an unburdening,
an unrelenting love
that cannot be explained.

Trying to untie the ego,
the knot of human existence,
I breathe in pain,
I breathe out love.

I transmute what is.
I transform what was.

Rx for Connection

A Tattooed Promise

Trust what you don't know . . .
   —Kelli Russell Agodon

If we are all holding
the many-handled rope of pre-school in life,
then maybe the connecting, nylon fiber threads
are what is keeping us from falling off the earth.
Or, perhaps, we are all held together
by the spider web clinging
between the wooden beams of the house,
as delicate as lace,
as vulnerable as a ribcage—
the hope living within it.

We are woven love
and too many stitches.
We are thumbprints of trust,
every line a tattooed promise
that we will persist,
our kind will keep existing,
forever pointing to our birthplace
among the stars.

A Lemon Light Embrace

inspired by the painting Anastomosis *by Danelle Rivas*

We are wired for connection.
We walk on living land.
Soil in our veins,
butterfly wings painting our palms
with heart line and life line.
The green of every living thing
exists in the grass beneath our feet.
Life swims to our fingertips.

We reach out to touch robin's egg blue,
in love with the energy of air,
the pulsing rush of lifeblood
that comes with each savored breath.
Walk gently in meadows,
leave no mark on your life's hike,
wash sorrow from the terrain
by removing bottles,
wrappers, and the debris of modern living.

Cocoon yourself in moments,
in the rise and fall of nature's chest
that swells and falls just to release
oxygen for us all.
Hold close each and every tiny living thing.
Offer your hand like a mountain peak,
like a tree branch,
like a true offering of refuge.
Be the safe place for nature to flourish,
as you have been nurtured,
embraced by a lemon-hued light.

You Are Earth

You are not living on Earth. You are Earth.
Nature is not matter only. She is also spirit.
—Carl Jung

You are the pulse of the soil's veins.
You are the wriggling earnestness of the worm.
Water shoots up your stems.
You stand tall, leaves fanning out,
a glistening, life force energy.

A connected universe of intricate patterns,
human, plant, mammal, fish—
our hands embrace all elements
as we exist from root to tip
within branch song,
within the river's melody.

We hold life in our arms,
in our palms,
in our open wound hearts.

You are every star's last burst of light.
You are cosmos and ocean floor creature.
You are the smallest cell that begins
with nothing but the will to expand
and grow exponentially.

Your feathered form
once came from another land.
Your soul's birthplace waits for your return to source.
Until that sacred reunion,
let the clouds tremble with your thunder,
let the grass know you feel every brush of skin.
Feel the world, hold tenderly the globe.

Slumber Song

with a line from T.S. Eliot

The quiet song of your breath
is a meditation for morning.
The rise and fall of your chest
is the soft pillow I rest on,
unwilling to move from the dream
that is now,
the stillness of this moment.

I sink further,
feel the contact points of my body
become heavy with sleep.
Like a patient etherized upon a table,
every limb is numb, unable to move.
The cat stretches, sun glows golden
through the window.
We gently stir.

The music of wind and rain
dancing upon the windows
moves us into action.
We struggle to arise, watch squirrels
do their busy work of gathering,
greet fall with curiosity,
a season interrupting our milky slumber.
I rub the smoky haze of indifference
from my eyes,
see clearly through the freshly washed windows
of tomorrow.
I wait patiently for the quiet song
of your breath to return,
my place of welcomed rest.

Uncertain Feet

We are living in the now time
of uncertain feet
and tissue paper plans.
To see beyond requires a willingness
to hold the railing,
when we don't know where
the stairs lead.
So, we stand 6 feet apart,
take comfort in the small things
we can share,
like the recipe for lentil soup
or a photo of wildflowers
on our morning walk.
How odd to move forward
when it feels like
we're on a bridge to nowhere.
The secret is simply to move
every day and remember how
our hands once connected in greeting.
We will touch palms again.

A Love Song in the Key of Blue

inspired by Interior with a Violin Case *by Henri Matisse*

Blue notes of seascape and
twilight love surround me.
The missing violin
sings inside my chest.
The empty case of sound
holds space for our seasoned love—
the love that walks on the beach
with no words,
the love that breathes a sigh
in recognition that it is time to sleep,
the love that looks in a mirror,
sees our passing, weathered years in reflection
as the gift that it is,
rather than the slow burn
of youth escaping our fingers.

All gentleness lives
within the violin's horsehair threaded bow,
the graceful ribbon smoothing all sound,
the quiet melody permeating the air
and rising, rising to waiting clouds,
the billowing cushions that receive
every sweet nothing whispered,
and remembered,
the heavens where our love is recorded
on parchment,
in the handsewn book of us,
that will never be told again
in quite the same way,
an imprint of our unique souls
in dulcet tones and ink.

A Split Second Embrace

Warming my hands
on a mug of Rishi rooibos tea,
I watch the steam rise,
then follow my natural gaze
out the 2nd floor window
of Rochambo Coffee & Tea House.

Three friends appear on the street corner.
They zoom in for a group hug,
arms wide open, a flourish of wings.

Don't look down, look up,
I think. *Look out, look beyond.*
It is a split second embrace.
My eyes catch the moment,
rest there, witness the grace
of togetherness from my perch,
like a curious owl.

I put my phone away,
close the magazine I am reading,
open up my journal
and then close that, too,
after capturing a few lines.

I sit at the table
looking out,
climb out of my brick apartment of self
and sink more deeply into the
billowing expanse of white clouds—
feel myself rising.

Life Becomes

The way the sun
greets your skin with warmth,
the curve of your son's smile
after he finishes a pen and ink sketch,
the feel of water on your toes
when you first step into the ocean,
the release of breath after sharing a hard truth,
the slip of silk on the tongue
with the first bite of your mother's
egg custard dessert,
the scent of fried clams
on that first night of vacation—
oh, the anticipation of it—
the sound of church bells on the hour,
how you recognized the melody
every time you visited home,
the lengthening sigh when a sunset deepens
to a tawny red,
then bursts into orange,
just at the edge of vision.
This is how your life becomes a poem.

About the Author

Cristina M. R. Norcross lives in Wisconsin with her husband and two sons. She is the founding editor of the online poetry journal, *Blue Heron Review,* and the co-founder of Random Acts of Poetry and Art Day (celebrated annually on February 20th). Author of nine poetry collections, a multiple Pushcart Prize nominee, and an Eric Hoffer Book Award nominee, her most recent book is *The Sound of a Collective Pulse* (Kelsay Books, 2021). Cristina's poems have been published widely in online and print journals including: *Lothlorien Poetry Journal, The Poet, Muddy River Poetry Review, Verse-Virtual, The Ekphrastic Review, Poetry Hall, Visual Verse, Silver Birch Press,* and *Pirene's Fountain,* among others. She has also been published in numerous print anthologies. Cristina has helped organize community art and poetry projects, has led creative writing workshops, and has hosted many open mic readings. She facilitates the online writing prompt group, Connection & Creativity in Challenging Times, on Facebook. Cristina was featured in the Poem-A-Day series for the Academy of American Poets in 2021. Most recently, you can find her work in the James Crews anthology, *The Wonder of Small Things* (Storey Publishing, 2023), alongside notable poets, Ada Limón, Joy Harjo, Ted Kooser, Jane Hirshfield, Kimberly Blaeser, Mark Nepo, Natalie Goldberg, Ross Gay, and others.

Find out more at
www.cristinanorcross.com

www.ingramcontent.com/pod-product-compliance
Lightning Source LLC
Chambersburg PA
CBHW022144160426
43197CB00009B/1421